I0080965

Mbera

Mbera

poems by

Rethabile Masilo

CANOPIC
PUBLISHING

Canopic Publishing
601 Indigo Lane
Woodstock, IL 60098
www.canopicpublishing.com

Copyright © 2024 by Rethabile Masilo.

All rights reserved under International and Pan-American Copyright Conventions. Published in the United States by Canopic Publishing, Woodstock, Illinois.

Cover design by Sarah Hasty Williams
Author photo by Sabine Dundure

ISBN-13: 978-0-9997182-6-1

Preface

Forenames in Lesotho almost always have a meaning. Our eldest sibling, a sister, is named Kananelo, or "acceptance." Our brother, the first-born son, was named Khotsofalang, or "be satisfied." He died circa 1979 at the hands of the then-Lesotho government and rogue elements of its army. A couple of years before we were attacked, Khotsofalang left home to join the overthrown Basotho Congress Party (BCP) government, then in exile, and get training and education to be able to return home and fight against—and remove from power—the illegal government that had been ruling with a rough hand since 1970 when it had lost the general election but decided to stay in power by force nevertheless. I'm the third born, a boy. My forename means "we are happy." Our sister who comes after me is Tokoloho, or "freedom." Self-explanatory, since we were a British protectorate at the time of her birth, and most folks were dreaming of freedom. Last is our youngest natural brother, Tšoanyane, a name that has been in our family for generations. No meaning of which I am aware. Our nephew Motlatsi ("added one") joined our family as an adopted brother a few years before 1981, the year of the attack.

Since the 1970 coup that overthrew the BCP, leaders and other active members of the BCP had been jailed, and the ones not in jail were either harassed, tortured or killed. In a way, because of this, it was a cynical type of good luck that our father, Benjamin Masilonyane Masilo, had been one of the early ones to be rounded up and imprisoned. I was nine years old when it happened, and I remember three or four army 4x4s driving up to our home in Moshoeshoe II, a suburb of Maseru (the capital of Lesotho). They later left with Dad, after having ransacked our house hoping to find a reason to imprison him.

Our father spent a year and a half in jail. We did get to visit him every Saturday, and Mom would have fresh clothing and Tupperware containers of home cooking for him. They would talk about us, our schooling, and about the difficulties Mom was going through. Among other concerns, she had five children on her hands with car and house payments to see to while being jobless. We lived in extreme poverty. Khotsofalang, nicknamed Mbera, was deeply moved by the whole experience. And while we all were affected, I think for Mbera it was a quasi-daily specter that slowly gnawed at him. During this time he unwittingly coined his nickname himself. Wanting to show his classmates that we weren't poor, he filled a sort of cheque with thousands of rands (the local currency then), scribbled his name in as the beneficiary, signed it 'Mbera.' He showed it to his friends and told them it was from our Uncle Mbera. We had never had an uncle with that name. When he was debunked, the nickname stuck.

After Dad had been released from prison and had found a job in South Africa (but based in Lesotho), Mbera asked him, "How come you and the leaders of our party aren't doing anything to remove this illegal government?" Unbeknownst to our brother, the BCP in exile was already in the process of developing armed resistance in the form of a military wing called The Lesotho Liberation Army (LLA). I don't recall what Dad said, but Mbera was not satisfied. He often mentioned wanting to leave the country to study abroad, if he could obtain a studentship. At Peka High School, where we were both boarders and played football, he and his friends started selling loose cigarettes, oranges and apples. When I inquired why, he said it was for extra pocket money. It turned out that the money collected was for his group of friends to have the means to skip the country to Botswana to join that nascent resistance. The following is how it panned out.

One evening, when we were home for the holidays, Mbera exposed their plan to me. He told me that they would be taking a train the next morning for Gaborone, the capital of Botswana. I remember saying, "I'll come with you." But his face hardened, and he said that I was not ever going anywhere with them. "Imagine if we both didn't return. Imagine what that would do to Mom," he said. And the case was closed. The next morning when everyone was wondering where he was, I acted as surprised as they were. It is important to note that I have never regretted not telling our parents about the boys' plan. When word got out and the parents of the 'missing' children started comparing notes, it was confirmed that they were in Botswana. Some parents promptly left to go and bring their children back while others, like mine, did not. And I understood and still understand their decision. I only told my parents years later what I had known but had kept to myself.

As the eldest son, Mbera was the head of our family and he had made a daring decision for which we respected him. And now, as the second son, I am the head of our family and one of the only things I can do is honour him, honour his memory, and honour his sacrifice. We still don't know how he died. We still don't know where he died. We still don't know when he died. His body was never given to us. So, we can only estimate that he died two or three years before 4 September 1981, at about four a.m., when the Lesotho Government sent a mob of rogue army elements (nicknamed Koeeoko, basically a killing squad. Koeeoko is Sesotho for water-snake) to assassinate our father. Mr Mofo Odilon Seheri had already been killed. On 21 June 1981, his calcined bones and car were found atop a mountain. The only way to identify him was with his wedding ring. Dad was second on the list (at that time we did not know that Mbera was already dead. We only found out after fleeing the country). I'd rather describe what happened that night with a ghazal that appeared in my first book of poems, *Things that are silent* (Pindrop Press, 2015).

My father's killers

They take to the road at midnight and turn
Toward land that by right we plough and turn.
Their dark convoy passes white-washed houses.
A brake light: the bakkies slow down and turn.
They park at right angles to the street

To light the yard. It's daddy's day and turn.
They have come on a crisp September night
To blight us, make our season change and turn.
The moon shimmers its flashlight on a blade
While, from a height, the planets spin and turn.

They used machine guns to fire through the windows
of our parents' bedroom. At dawn our three-year old
nephew Motlatsi, who liked to sleep between our parents,
was confirmed dead, his body riddled with bullets. Dad
was nowhere to be found, while Mom was under their bed,
trembling but unharmed. Somehow Dad had slipped out of
an unguarded kitchen window and fled the country to South
Africa. We think that a compassionate member of the killing
squad looked the other way, for we can't imagine them not
having surrounded the house.

After the boy's funeral, Mom and I hatched a plan to
get the family out. We stuffed ourselves into the car (with no
luggage at all, in case we raised suspicion), and crossed the
frontier legally at the border post, the way we usually did when
going shopping in South Africa. This time we only returned
to Lesotho after a family exile of nine years in Nairobi, Kenya,
while my younger sister and I were in the USA at Maryville
College in Tennessee, furthering our studies. I met my wife,
Odile Ordibehesht Masilo there, and moved with her to France,
her home country. We have two children, Benjamin Thabo
Babak Masilo and Diane Lineo Roxane Masilo.

Khotsofalang was buried in absentia when the family
finally returned home. His spirit was added to the tomb of the
nephew he never knew. Khotsofalang's date of death on the
new, shared tombstone, is a question mark.

This book is dedicated to our brother, Mbera and, by
extension, to our parents, our siblings, our nephew, and the
people of Lesotho.

Rethabile Masilo
Paris 2024

Contents

I

George Stinney Jr.	13
Stop what you're doing	14
A dream about Mbera	15
Mbera quit school	16
Theoretic logic	17
Bleeding	18
Book	19
Cleansing	20
Leabua's face	21
Ladder	22
Leasing	23
Making a film	24
Mosotho child	25
My heart is empty now	26
Impersonal	27
Singing	28
The empty chair	29
We lived	30

II

Adieu to a steed	35
Deadweight	36
For my mother	37
In my house	38
Killing	39
Life	40
My mother says she sees him	41
Parents	43
Pickaxe	44
Scent	45
The bottom of the stack	46
The duck	47
The long cold	48
The nails of my father	49
Threnody for Sharpeville	50

III

Another world   53
Let the poem be a toddler   54
A tale of viruses   55
A wish   56
Beef   57
Inside the hill   58
Devil's weed & ginger   59
Going home after work   60
Mirrored   61
Corrida de toros   62
Reading   63
Lovers   64
On edge   65
The detective   66
The number of dreams   67
Three Women   68
The peace of silence   69
The stranger next to me   70
The visiting   71
When we die   72
Whiskey in the jar   73
For Peter Horn (1934—2019)   74

I

The war speaks at night
with its lips of shredded children

—Tyehimba Jess, 'Mercy'

George Stinney Jr.

The boy, at the height of his 14 years, sat on a big
book in an electric chair, like a foot in a parent's shoe,
thinking of the unknown, his legs not touching the floor
but his head shaved right for the helmet
to fit its inner curvature, sponge, and wire mesh.
Perhaps it was a Who's Who of the chief politicians,
judges and magistrates of the State; or a stack of Bibles
he was supposed to swear on with his arse. His parents
had instilled in him the ability to pray, the assurance
of heaven in the next world and beyond / but he was out
of prayers now, his tongue dry and full in his mouth
from repeating all the alleluias that a boy can say,
a boy who bore his father's name and his mother's face,
counting the seconds before the lever was pulled down
and electricity shot through his body and illuminated
the origins of his race / precious time. He remembered
when he was young, counting Mississippis during
a game of hide-and-seek. When the hangman pulled
the knob down George shut his eyes and said *one miss*

Stop what you're doing

a voice said from within, to them:
stop this now, and make instead room
for a new world—for creating space
was all the country could look forward
to. But they continued to prod and dig,
to reach the curvy part his heart lay in,
a heart like an egg in a deserted nest
that night we took off at the sound
of guns, and our flock flew northerly
above the vast, peaceful ocean, fleeing
fear, even as we left his heart in its chalice.
We told and told those men to leave him be,
to let his three-year old cadaver alone.
But people are what money makes them,
and they dug, dug and passed pickaxes
from hand to hand. And so, one day, when
the time comes, and they kill a baby girl,
will she start playing liketo in the cavity?
Will there be anyone to sing her to sleep?
This fury of night is harsh under the moon,
and makes darkness acclimatise to anything.
And though the soldiers are gone, now, arms
hanging like broken limbs at their sides,
gone home to make fresh anger and hone
new limbs, it is too late for the boy, down
there, feeding on Jesus's dandelions.

A dream about Mbera

Our brother trickled candle wax onto my cheeks as I slept,
then chased the other siblings with a sjambok into a donga
beyond the maize fields at the bottom of Qoaling,
where we lived. They hid behind buttresses
that keep dongas from caving in.
Always littered with tins, bottles, used rubbers—a toilet to many—
no donga ever gave a thing—they grab our soil
and drag it to dump in South Africa, as if that country
hadn't thieved enough already. In my last dream of him,
a drought had sapped parts of the donga walls,
and none of their ramparts were safe anymore.
I don't know what got into us, for everything that day
was like we were walking backwards into the past,
because we turned around and clambered into his car
which he sent fleeing down the street past the greying shop
of Mmamak'hoba, toward a gully—the brother we hadn't seen
in years, except when a dream made it possible for us to meet,
the boot of his car flapping like a cape behind us.
We flew over the edge into a ravine deep as the divide
that always kept us to ourselves, away from nemeses.
I awoke with thoughts of escape on my mind,
until I saw a sun leaking through cracks in the wall
in an afterlife that nobody recognizes, nor can heal.

Mbera quit school

and went to feed the revolution,
and soil, and trees, with blood;
people have snickered ever since,
as if the ones fat with life today
are lesions that will ever crust.

the body is proprietor of itself
but this they do not know, every
thing in the end does give way
and moves past the heart to hell.

nothing heals a life of betrayals
and of lone battles with the self,
like swallowing drums of spirits.

Theoretic logic

—As said to Aylan Kurdi

One theory says the sea sucked you in,
either that—or the dinghy pushed you,
saw you sink, asked your dad to carry you
to the shore before the sun lost every hope.
That same theory was never given a name.
The one of Realism says life is not theories,
it says something always goes wrong, or will,
which makes Murphy feel happy with himself.
How come the world allows this rush to feed
people to the earth with its delineated mouths
dug out from grounds near houses of prayer?
Religion makes an imam smear a bundle with
salve and put it in a vault big as a father's shoe.

The ones who saw it happen swear the waves
after they had regained consciousness flinched
in horror at the thought of touching you.

Bleeding

Dawn bleeds on the grounds
of the main house in Qoaling
and goes from there to every room
of the house, clinging to lineages
and threads plaited into our 'fros
with a few, frayed fibres of hope
born of those felled in mid-sleep,
those who were never afraid
to furnish hope, and re-enter
shadows, and conquer them.

Book

Go into a book
and in it find a place to sit.
Afterward you will feel on your skin
breath the fleshless send
from the bellows of nostrils
into your life.
Let the memory of life
deaden every spirit.
Burn, but remember
that it is not important
to know the name of the tome you're in,
and may forever roam,
the same way you don't know
the name of your home
but take refuge in it
against battles with the city,
each time you hear the death
squad march up the road...

Cleansing

We repainted the inner walls of our house in Qoaling
with ineffaceable paint.
First, we rendered the holes left there by a night of anger,
sandpapered them,
the way someone might scrub sin off their skin, to find
what could help dispel the legacy of those days.
Then we held a ritual over the spot where he had lain.

In the morning, as the sun climbed behind Lithabaneng,
we unglued the linoleum in his bedroom,
carried it outside like firefighters holding a life net,
rolled it into an old oil drum to burn it, and watched
its toxicity billow up and disappear, like some smoke-signal,
toward the one who allows such things to happen.

After that, because it had been like removing a part of oneself
that no longer worked, we sat down and shared rusks
and stories about him, without mentioning his name.
It was like a rite, though the intention was never to turn it into
a sad event. We convinced ourselves that it was a celebration

of the name we could not say of the one who was gone. Then
we rose, cleaned and painted the walls of his room, for we had
left the grounds and the lebala, in front of the house, for late
afternoon when it would be cooler, never having said his name once,
nor those of the men who visited our house that September night.

Leabua's face

We used to spot Leabua in the window of a limousine.
They'd dismiss school so we could wait for his car to pass
And wave at him with paper flags they would hand out.
They never showed us Mbera's face, if they burned him.
Although Moshoeshoe's sister died at the end of January,
Nineteen-seventy, hands of memory bring stuff to us—
The names of cattle bled at funerals. So many funerals
Their lowing is still loud near the limits of the abysses.

From a father's blemished hands, the soft ones of a mother,
The arms of every elder who came before—all will always
Bring us the past: a photo with the boy in it, every hand
On deck eating minutes of time, making sure our brother
Is the perfect picture of our dream. When you think about it,
About the different faces that have lost all sharp contour,
All edge… is it a blessing, or is it a curse above all else?
Then the time I dreamed about our nephew's lifeless face.

Ladder

I am a child learning to steal a boat
to steer from Boston home to Anyama,
on the back of a night gleaming
with fear that its lights might be seen,
how escapees would shut eyes, mouths, ears
and stopped thinking for lengths of time
to keep the brightness in, holding their breath
too long sometimes, eyes flushed with worry,
during every fleeing quest for liberty,
women and men with bone-white teeth
against the wine of their gums but whose
laughter was packaged in themselves
in everglades around the feet of mangroves
and even before, in rows of cotton plants.
Yet, look at them now, there on a top step,
lengthening the side-rails and adding rungs
to a ladder to bring others up and lend
a hand to the past, send the elevator down
to lift even more, the way Ms Tubman did.
Look at them, these whose forebears hid
from dogs and moved in the night like fish
through muddy waters. *Look at them now.*

Leasing

Of all the boys on that rock playing
morabaraba, he was the leased one,
lent by the gods for a secret reason.
He was always ahead of the rest,
even unto death. Who'd have known
that anyone's future could be shot?

The year kept its intent secret from us,
till in the strangest chapter of the hour,
Khotsofalang was dead. They had dragged
him up down Kingsway through town
to dissuade other pupils of democracy.

I discuss this under the state of a planet
that is silent as a grave. I am custodian
of a world whose locks open only from
out to in, bodies trapped all the way in
a ritual whose law entombs the dead.

Making a film

The moment mother comes in with the rest of the children
we huddle at the centre of the room
and wait for another shooting,
especially that it's late and the village is asleep.
Maybe we're already dead.
The pain in this is how a parent says
it hurts them more to thrash a child
and straighten the life in them than it does the child.
Like mud that has slid from a mountain after a storm
and now waits at the delta below—calm as a child
who has finished crying. That's what happened to us.
When Mbera walks in, carrying our nephew in his arms,
a dozen lights shoot from eyes that seek to connect,
until morning pulls out of its pocket a kaleidoscope
of every feeling. Like a spirit, a searchlight
follows our father the way it did the night he fled,
angry bullets pursuing him. He moves
closer to his wife and they vanish into air, even
as our small group strives to understand.
There's no sound in the room, or outside, no tangent feeling,
but just at that instant a reaching for the other.
Nothing to diminish the moment.
We all think that the moon saw and registered everything.
That's why there will never be need for a trailer or a spoiler
for our film, made the night after those men came.
It's credit crawl shows the names of everyone
who was present on that day it happened,
in our house at the foot of a hill in Qoaling, where
we lived, died, were unable to make our ghosts
agree to leave the new occupants alone.

Mosotho child

Sometimes, even after the sun has gone
and street music has stirred the town
and tired the people,
but there are dancers still
from neighbouring villages
laughing and draining their beers,
I do not leave my room.
My world is in walls of words.
I study shadows that crawl down the hillside
like let blood setting, before making the choice
to go back to my people, to the eyes
of those who fathomed the world
and brought it the revolt of peace,
moulded it, according to the needs
of its people, conjured everything up
and constructed it for lives to come,
kneading soft its clay.

My heart is empty now

Please, let me just turn down this volume in my head
and sit back, place my hands behind my head
like a hammock around an ailing body—
though where I shall go from there I do not know.
Where does one go when the heart is empty, even
as a mind reels with the persistence of love?
A dove crosses the city and arcs into its distance.
A plane carrying halves of people coasts overhead. Soon
they'll join themselves at their destination,
the way you and I tore bills of money in half
and kept a piece each, the last day before school,
then scotched them back during holidays when we reunited,
changed by distance and boarding school. We grew
into men apart, and always became children again, till
it was time to part once more. My heart is empty now.
I shut my eyes, watch you (on the screens behind
their lids)—determined one morning—grab your bag
and walk out down the path past the football field.

Impersonal

They came to our house one night
to pound its doors with boots. Spring
will never forget how we refused to weep
to keep their system going. How could we
forgive the way they nodded in agreement
to the impulse of killing us? We have
dreaded sleep ever since. But it was not
personal, they say, it was impersonal.
Something our father had done, something
that was never in the press nor on the radio.
A secret sin known only to the ones in boots
and those who pay them to be straight-faced.
Fear clasped our throats with cold fingers
and squeezed. We had never loved its name
nor hung out with it nor laughed with it
at the expense of a child's gasp, never told it
the story of what makes us stay in our self,
whether or not night brings its silence.
You are all meaning. All meaning is you.
From then, time has shown its face of rot.

Singing

You can't run away from yourself
—Bob Marley

What she is singing I don't know, on a street so long,
like a corridor with tall walls—no one knows
what her song means, and we show no interest in it—
yet with her small child voice she sings the song
like a hymn. Why are you singing this, I say. She looks
at me and sings about my clothes and the look of my face
and this climate that is getting ready to fall,
and goes on about my vehicle, the house I live in.
When I look up, the answer from the sky is tears
of the kind she has been singing about.

The empty chair

I find this chair—in a forest—to which rays direct light,
a chair to the back of which a crow-coloured gamp is tied,
like a big bat landing, even as whispers keep saying
she is not coming back... from spaces deeper in the woods.
But I am a parent, and I sense a child sitting there, as if
strapped by some blunder of justice to an electric chair,
and as much out of curiosity as from love, I pluck from the air
a first molecule I am allowed to touch by hand and place it,
then a next, molecule by molecule until in the going light
I begin to see her nose, then its nostrils. She breathes in
and breathes out, and I form her lips, cheeks, carefully
like someone interlacing yarn and thread into a rug
while nearly holding their breath. I glue her together
in that chair and watch her watch me build the rest of her,
till morning arrives, in the daydream of whose promise
pearls of frost cling to her, a girl in sparkling jodhpurs
holding a lunge whip, glowing in that forest like a spook.
But knowing curiosity, my taste for discovery, I knew
I was going to stay till night with her, to craft, out of air,
a semblance of her horse my hands were dying to make.

We lived

in that house when we did,
        where those who never had
                couldn't have known our truth,
                        why the rooms had it in for us.
Qoaling sprawled down a hill
        like a police body outline.
                One day, when the time was ripe,
                        a hackney carriage pulled up
and parked outside our house
        with its cargo of whatever things
                each of us had accomplished,
                        everything we had done
or failed to do, and it waited
        with its empty silence outside,
                the horses wet with sweat
                        and starting to nibble our grass
and shudder, following their trip
        across parched woods which
                used to be the dreadlocks
                        of the heads of our kingdoms.
When our lineage was young,
        every mother would sparkle
                just like the water they fetched
                        from early morning springs,
drew out of the ground and bring it
        home to their sleeping families.
                Inside our house that day we put
                        our belongings together
into trunks made of motsepele wood
        which used to grow thick
                around these environments,
                        but no more. When we left
there was no sound,
        not until we hit the streets
                down near the periphery,
                        and met bureaucrats there

who weigh people's hearts
       on small, modern balances
              that with quantum accuracy
                    calculate the magnitude
of evil inside a terrified, fleeing
       human being. We prayed
              for one thing and one thing
                    only—for the value of good
in us to counterweigh
       our basest acts. Neighbours
              looked on from along dirt streets,
                    waving to us with hands
like small flags, not knowing
       that we would come back
              and bring with us all the truth,
                    and live in our old house again.

II

I will stand in the center with my fellow scarecrows
and chant against the darkness

—Geoffrey Philp, 'Shlomo's Return'

Adieu to a steed

When a steed dies, I cut off
its tail and comb the length of it,
saw off its hooves and with a spoon
scoop all the gristle out of them.
And that's not all. With the tail
I make a fly swish for my uncle,
who is often at war in life as he is
in the sickness of death today.
Out of the four emptied hooves
I make keratin ashtrays for him.
He's wrestling with TB so much
his friends mimic his long rasps
and say, 'Nthaha, TB or not TB?'
He starts laughing at himself
until into his fist he is coughing
the blood-red river of revolt.

Deadweight

This park in which I'm lying now with my eyes closed
is very quiet. I am near the source of all indifference.
Sometimes I can make roots out whispering to each other
(like humpback whales in the distance), small whiskers
against the skin of my face, the weight of the world on me.
Perhaps it's because I miss my children, whom life took me
from. Perhaps because I'm all alone here and it is quiet
but for the incessant chirping of red bishops in the trees,
the flutter of their life, a distant noise of creatures inside
my head, roots breathing, searching the loam of a world
with their fingers. I think I have been here I don't know
how long—time slackens after a while, the clock's stroke
slows enough for one to mostly hear each of them screech
across a coarse blackboard, as time continues to put on
the brakes to a calamitous life. Sometimes I strain to see
what is being written, but all is black. My mind is blank.
I just hear chalk zigzagging, yet I find it interesting
that I have reached a level of peace that requires no food
or other form of sustenance. It is only love that I miss,
laughter loud as the voice of a cave. And that is what
I know everybody will be deprived of in the hereafter.

For my mother

Like a face assembling its brow into a frown,
the atmosphere outside gathers—not out of anger
but out of understanding what is inevitable.
The first, few flakes of sleet are on the way;
the house is starting to chill, to ready
for a post-mortem. The dog was restless last night,
whimpering in its kennel and sobbing like a child,
because yesterday's errors make tomorrow's new day.
They say what was built on terror must end in grief,
until the sky opens its arms like a mother when a child
gets home. I feel no life in my body anymore
when I watch my mother's sipping tea.
She no longer stands beside the kitchen sink
in sheep slippers. She goes early to bed. I steal
to her room to check for breath. Afternoon clouds
hanging above look like the hoary hair of ancestors
with their lifetimes turned upside down, yes,
and with their angriest rain about to pour.

In my house

Here is why in my house
when relief is absent,
and windows are open
to the silence outside,
there is always, alive in
each corner of the rooms,
the company of forebears—
one, in the form of bedrock,
carries offspring in its arms
and walks with a limp
to avoid fuel lamp flames
setting its dress on fire.
Another, a foundation,
is quiet except for a grunt
when the weight is great
and rain refuses to fall,
and souls leave their cloaks
near the door and go to sleep,
and wait for day, clothes
on the floor near the door.
Above a window a boy
waits, bow and arrow
ready in his fleshy hands.
And when noise finally
filters in from the street
memory closes its eyes,
and that is when I enter
each room on the balls
of my feet and to touch
each corner with the tips
of my fingers to feel for
sore spots and lacerations.

Killing

Chauvin kills the way my grandfather did, by choking
the last, stifled breath in a goat's throat with his knee,
before cutting its neck with a knife,
in the evening on a sultry day in May, before dinner,
its bleats of *I-can't-breathe!* caught in the gullet of its throat.
My grandfather's knee was deaf to pleas—there was food
to put on the table.
                  The legs were first... then the whole body
fidgeting, its appeals enough to remind one of somebody
squirming on the side of a road. On my way home after work
I saw a guy die, and the asphalt said it'd happen again
and again, and again, and again, and again, and again,
in Amerika where the police work in slaughterhouses.

Life

When at peace, feeling like the best of your body,
it is impossible to imagine some muscle twitching,
wrecked by the increase in years, a shoulder loose
every time you run for the bus, God inching nearer
with each tremor of the hand, though it will not be
till the lungs draw dust in and your voice rasps,
as in a hopeless dream, that you will understand
how evil all of this is, after a ligament has waned
and atrophied. And if ever the flank gives, you pray
for release from terror that makes you recall
past acts, and you ask your family to find the courage
to bring Doctor Death to your bedside.
You don't like the urine balloon tied to your waist.
You never wanted to die with tubes up your nose.
Besides, how cruel is it to let somebody rot,
when they used to wear their body so sensual?

My mother says she sees him

She said... I see him outside
in that area beyond the house.
It must have been the yellow in her eyes.
She has had time since he left
to scrub them into clear marbles,
and allow saltwater to rinse them,
but the yellow has stayed, like rust
on an abandoned freshwater pipe.
When we were young, she would see
into our childish dreams with them,
in the unforgiving dark.
He stands there bent at the waist,
refusing to crack or to break,
and she describes his teeth, clenched
like a beast holds in its jaws
a wriggling body by the thew,
in the dim light beside the door.
She sees this with her marbles.
They couldn't break him when
they hauled him off in cuffs, after
searching our house and bringing years
of its ceilings down. They wouldn't
break him, later when they refused us
the body of his son they had killed.
He holds the rife murder of his son
in the mouth between his teeth.
After the storm he came back, added
muscle to his limbs, arms, legs,
to the tree trunk of his neck.
Nothing cold-hearted or immoderate
but an annual ring each year
added to his bole—as he grew roots
deep as an icicle that finally enters earth
with each new drop of blood that creeps
down the path of life. That's how

when his frozen months arrived, he dug in.
It made him live, made him get back
to hoeing his country of youth, a plot
of Qoaling where people, like sequoia trees,
tower over the roof of a forest and care for
its soul. That is what my mother said.

Parents

Our mother loved our father like we loved both.
Sometimes they'd circle each other on Sundays
like peacocks, strutting before or after church
with Eden in their eyes because fruit
had been discerned, picked, relished, first
by her, then—in a move by a man who, in love
as in battle, fought with feeling—by him out of
her hand, eating it with his eyes closed.
Our parents knew what was coming that night
but they stayed up to wait for the droning sound
of car engines along a road where cars never passed
at four in the morning. Qoaling stretched
all the way down to the Main Road that led
from Borokhoaneng to the south of the country.

Pickaxe

There was a time when blood was not necessary,
and a man could work a pickaxe into terrain
cracked into clods by a drought of nectar,
bleeding nothing from its body but paving for rain,
digging, going home in the evening with arms
drained from swinging a pick and striking dirt.

Today we walk around still waiting for rain
that never comes, hands hanging. Soil never dies.
Something always brings it a new beginning,
whether it's early in the continuum of life or late.
Earth finds a way, the sprig of a black-face song
in its teeth, pushing demise back on its knees.

The sound of an older man breathes below a window
at a manor inside which age is asleep. He comes out
and stands before the crowd with his ageless head,
bent on letting death know that its end is near.
You can tell his grip is firm, and when the pickaxe
flashes, the crowd moves back, holding its breath.

He's the father of the father of the son and grandson
they came for and took away. His wife still goes
to the well every morning when spring water is clear,
when it is not yet time for anyone else to be up readying
day—before a sun shines fresher meaning on them.

Scent

The gods had never treated us this way—no,
they had never sent us away from our land
or performed surgery on our hearts
nor on any part of the bodies of people we love,
a body being the hand-me-down ancestors give.
It is certain that they had never done this to us,
for what reward would they get from such a thing?
When the voice of my grandmother finds me
it wobbles about how like the sense of memory
everything is failing this world, she keeps saying
that we should bottle memory, like scent, in that
characteristic tremor of old people's voices.
The sweat of terrified people in a urined corner.
She says that after sinning even if we scrubbed
our hands like Pilate we would still be guilty,
guilty as charged, wearing blankets of remorse
in a country closest to heaven than all others.
No, the gods have done nothing to make us
forget to serve each other heaping spoonfuls
of ubuntu every day. *When the time is right, die,*
she says. *Not scared, but with hope in your eyes.*

The bottom of the stack

I will never forget how our mother
dragged a heated iron comb through her hair,
taking out kinks that used to adorn heads of queens
and kings, with the hope of ironing out her life.
My father ran the hundred yards and did well—
picked the shotput up with his hands,
like a cannonball, and put it on his shoulder,
saying nothing all the while.
He never whined when the Englishman
looked down on him on the street or at work.
He would type letters, draft articles for the office
and classify them, as he continued
to swallow his bile, which he later put
at the bottom of the stack but in a separate file.
He chased the English from Lesotho and was stunned
when the country turned and trained its guns on him.
One day we found his bile-file while spring cleaning.

The duck

A duck glides across the surface of a pond
leaving an avenue for its children to follow.
It has a locomotive you do not see, as with posture
and its head on that ribboned neck
it skims from one side like a skater to another.
A man next to me says... it's a woman.
Not a girl, not a boy, not a man? I ask. How do you know?
Did you look under her skirt? And I giggle alone.
Mothers know how to labour and make it seem
graceful, he adds. *For under the surface, with pistons*
like those of a potent, powerful car, she's paddling
like heck. (I contemplate a slave fleeing
the cottonfields to a place of liberty, Tubman
slashing bramble with a cutlass and leaving a trail
for the children of her people to follow).

The long cold

Some of the men I did eat, while others
I discarded, pushed them aside in my plate like peas,
small night shooters who came with their equipment
to shoot slumber out of our dreams.
I sought those who were genuinely great,
who carried themselves like bison steaks.
I needed to eat them.

A stone's throw from September fourth
tall molutu trees stood strong against spring gusts
one usually must battle with, their bark
dark from the long cold.

I'd noticed how my father crunched bones
and sucked the marrow of a government,
how he laughed and talked politics with his mouth full.
I was resolved to be the same.

They'd wave a carrot in his face
and he'd grab it and whack them with it.
He didn't care. He wanted meat,
the flesh of human rights bleeding
from the sacrificial life of thousands, the freshly cut
thew of his son who had begun to grow
enough to be as strong as those same trees.

Eat and wash it all down with umqombothi,
he used to quip. He was serious. He was a cannibal
and his vegetables came from bodies of men.

The nails of my father

Because I have my father's nails, I am afraid
of what I might do to complicate my life,
the way he pissed our government off,
then bared his teeth at it. The ends of my fingers
are hard and brittle like my father's.

Having his nails means I will have to die
at the hands of men, a point that knows no bounds—
die and enter the rigour of my body.

He was our father, and he knew,
because his nails were not whittled,
that he would live the way few do.

Threnody for Sharpeville

Mother says white people were once us.
She says they left, returned, that coming back
was the only thing on their minds,
before hurling herself at the sky
as if she was going to catch it,
touch the soles of God, grab a dead leg
and bring it back here, the opposite
of where a starved hawk takes its prey.
Ma says salmon know when their predator is near
because they smell themselves on its breath.
Like a hawk she leapt, my mother,
and if the world could turn upside down
her fingers would touch something,
someone's son, daughter, mother, father,
and bring them back here among us again.

III

For the boys and girls who grew in spite of these things
to be man and woman.

—Margaret Walker, 'For my people'

Another world

Distance is pleasure to feet. I walk up and down these streets
so long as their snow touches my face with its fingers, as if
the street was a form of penitence. Night has its shadows,
the people I pass cast theirs across my monumental shape,
like they know I left in the basement where this all began
your letters on a shelf, with the faces of their stamps
shocked at the speed at which the years move on,
around the time when our road was plain, and we found
distractions everywhere, like the day we did it in the Y
of a tree and you plucked a plum and ate it till you came.
I like the night. I like how it grows and beyond it
trees flock in shadows of furious birds. I move among them
with the hand of your snow brushing my face.
We were always looking for distractions, and one day,
at the end of evening, you took me down to the cemetery,
to encounter stone's suspended light. Silence rustled dead leaves,
a forest of marble occupied our mind, gave it form, banyan
piercing the layer of our upper world with its stem, pondering
two who loved among its trunks. A boneyard is no place for death.
The unbreathing are a world waiting to rise again. You hold me
in your hand and knead until the dead, aroused, thump
the roofs of their graves. I like the night, its time, black
with the glimmer of oil. The dark meaning of another world.

Let the poem be a toddler

on a bed, unable to surpass or surprise.
You are the one who makes this possible—
who wakes in the middle of night to shuffle around
humming to the child in your arms—you are
the one who calms, makes a sort of peace
with its head. Sometimes you must turn
gabble into meaning for life to get peace,
or dress the poem with matching socks and blouse
and take it out, in a pram, to show it off.
Or clothe it in shouting colours
to shock passers-by on the street, folks
used to reading road signs and sound bites only.
A child is unable to do any of these alone.
When it gets sick and you have, in a park sandpit,
a baby bawling for... you never know what... you scramble
to find an ailment, which you spray something on,
or feed it cough syrup, or sift through remedies
until you find the proper one
which you administer till the poem relaxes,
opens its mouth, swallows your labour in a yawn
and sleeps, so you may sleep too until the next day.

A tale of viruses

At the edge of my yard lived a footpath's end
where I came face-to-face with dawn, creeping on feet
fairies prance with from blade to blade of grass,
when they greet the world with their light,
till dawn's line reached me, stalled, announced itself,
waited for the guarantee of my promise.
Its fairies had just miraculously become gnomes
which brought my calm the noise of a world in pain,
bees having returned from their morning shopping spree.
I turned around and headed to the bungalow, daybreak
clamouring behind me, the stench of gnome breath
in my nose as a truck clattering toward the churchyard,
shook the road with its load of bubonic carcasses.
TV screens screamed their obliterating news to life,
tolls from prior days about the hole in the world.
The strangest thing was when, from my veranda,
I watched the gnomes morph into an array of viruses,
then march toward me and beyond, grumbling
of things germs must do, as they wriggled north
out of eye shot, past hives where bees sang songs
of blooms of poppies, before what the world had become.
Then I saw the woman again, a clay pail on her head,
her breasts firm, pass the edge of my yard on her way
from the well, and knew she knew we could feel cattle
lowing for the pasture, though there were no more cows.
Since I didn't care anymore, I let myself stir at her beauty,
alone on a path that promised to take us everywhere,
and make us feel we had not been disowned by life,
standing on my veranda, contemplating the universe.

A wish

When I die, I want to be buried face
down, so I can push with my shoulders
and the muscles in my upper arms
when, some day, I reject death, to be
like a plant piercing loam with its cotyledons.
To train for it, I crawl under our bed
and do push-ups with the sleeping world on me,
then wait for a next day. I've learned to keep
the tortoise of my spine curved, for my wish
is to carry the burden. I guess the loneliness
in children picking wildflowers is for my grave
for Father's Day and for all All-Saints Days.

Perhaps the wings I plucked off a fly when I was ten
and made it race across a page to win its life,
or the sides of puppies I kicked, will add weight
to the melancholy of my final day, my baggage
a bag of earth mixed with the gravel of my ways.
Bury me with my belly down, I say to you now.
And if you can't, burn me, and keep me
on a mantel in an urn so I may stay with you,
till there is no more world for anyone to stay in.

Beef

I'm hoping that when the rooster descends from the rafters,
like a child off a parent's shoulders—though I may not be there
to see it, in the serenity of the lip of dawn—its head will go back
into its mother's womb. It will be after the days of suffering
when our children bear descendants with the offspring
of enemies, surviving in clusters of determined souls.

The reasons to scalp are countless as Sitting Bulls
and Crazy Horses entombed beneath ancestral lands.
They are as many as negroes stabbed in the back with bullets,
They are as scared as Vietnamese children fleeing down a road
with flames shrieking from their mouths.
They are as loud as the sound of an atom bomb, cosmic
as a mushroom cloud. Those are the reasons today.

The number of times death flies over Kurdish lands
is inscrutable, and makes this a combat to the end, matched only
by the number of grains of sand on the shores of Normandy.
The war is over, but the beach remembers and has vowed
to produce the best and coarsest sandpaper for their hearts.

Let this beef be against constructive engagement, Reagan's policy
for apartheid, the child of whose friends bears the latest enemies.
Let us dig a mass grave, divide the number of corpses inside it
by how many times we've been vandalised, displaced, wounded,
and then make that quotient the target of our beef.

Inside the hill

Then the two men at the top
back into the mist, and a door opens
behind a clump of scrubs at our level.
They must have known we were the trainees
sent to them by the rector of our lives—
they press a button on the façade to let us in.
We follow them through a crack into a hall
where music clings to the walls with the fingers
of its notes, as shadows dance lazily.
We move among them and morph with their vapour.
It takes time to remember everyone, but we see
childhood friends, the boy who lived down the road
and had died abruptly. Somebody poisoned him,
then the cops threw his father in jail and sjamboked
his mother. Vendors and teachers from our town,
till the music slides off the walls, jumps out a fissure,
and leaves us pondering the story of our name
in silence. When the *baas* walks in, we awake
with rakes and pitchforks in our hands.

Devil's weed & ginger

I need to wash you from me, scrub your smell off,
though no matter what soap I use you do not go,
you are in me throughout and on me night and day
since the last time we touched, and even longer
after I ate you and felt you writhing against me.
Turn those hours to days, and those days to weeks,
then multiply the weeks by fifty-two several times:
that's how long I have remained with your absence.
I am an animal sniffing your essence to find my way
home. I remember how you relished it that last time.
We grew into each other, then were suddenly absent
from the years. I have been pounding devil's weed
and ginger from India and Ceylon in a clay mortar
to conjure you, dripping salt water on the blend
to try and keep your scent alive, stimulating me,
because I love it every time you melt over my face,
and me with a grin just going to die there forever.

Going home after work

She walks along the edges of a tube platform
as a train pulls in. I consider pushing her—
but the mind being what it is, I think
of the children she's likely to have, of how
she will look at their faces and smile at them
when the time is right for such a mood,
the husband she will spend Saturday mornings
sleeping in with, how like lock and key they'll fit,
their bodies curled like teardrops.

She will love the way he moans when his hands
study her. And because I understand this
I do not push her. As she passes, my mind
sees someone shoving Einstein to his death.

Mirrored

I saw you that evening in an alleyway
like a hatchling, your beak broken,
bird breath rasping at me.
I didn't talk to you for fear of the face I'd lose
if I stooped to lend you a wing, my mask off.
I feared how weak I'd seem—then
when I went back after passing a mirror in the hall
you were gone from where I'd seen you. I won't deny
I was relieved not to have had to drag you to my flat
near Montparnasse where neighbours watch
and scowl at such things—I won't deny I was fearful
of making them uncomfortable, that I was scared
to find myself in you. That I was loath to touch
both you and that rotting piece of foam
you call a bed. I won't deny I was afraid
to lose myself inside an act that may one day
contain what in many ways means me.

Corrida de toros

A shawn drags a tercio closer to the entrance,
until at last the priest appears.
He is fixing to prance for Olé, the blood god
of the sun. On this day,
a river of blood will be turned into water,
when he stabs the beast's hump
with his pike,
in the last minutes before the closing twirl.
A chain of passes, then a snap
of the muleta,
to piss the bull off and make it drop its hoist,
make it snort and paw and steam like a kettle,
shoulders wet with sweat,
their blades out like two raised hands,
the hide bright with oil,
which makes the congregation quake
and wander partway into their sermon fever,
as he shifts about the brute and then, neatly,
dances away, out of reach of an angry horn.
Upon smelling blood, the worshipers recall
a wedding at which water was turned to wine.
And their loins quiver with joy, at the vision
of blood turning into water. Only afterward,
when the sun leans into the Mediterranean
on its way west, does the priest change, out
of his thin cassock, to go home, a bull's ear
in each hand, tail dangling between his legs.

Reading

For one second you look at the audience,
then allow your eyes to drift back to the page
like the headlamps of cars that pass in the night,
so you can find where a next line fastens
to a previous thought in the text. And because
traffic is heavy you let your head bob up and down
as if you were agreeing to something, perhaps
to a voiced meaning of the road you're on,
or because faces in the rear are dark
and ache to hear and feel music ignite
with an intensity brighter than the lamp above
your head, illuminating a truth about the world,
as you pace yourself and never go beyond
the speed limit, reading each line with purpose
in your mouth, loud, or soft, like a requiem
when someone's sick, and mourners wait
at a hole in the ground wearing black, holding
oil lamps with their thoughts. You read on
to allow the dead to rest, the doe, motionless
on the side of the road. A swerve would have
saved her, had the lines not become frenzy
by themselves, lines as aslant as ropes of rain
on your windshield. You have told yourself
that this is how a poet reads lines,
so you stop looking at darkness and decide instead
to focus on each line, drive with your head down,
listening to the hum of the engine, like staring
at the central line when the lights aren't enough,
and following it to leave unknown territory.
Whoever heard of someone who's making love
look into the eyes of passers-by? Body sweat
covers you, withdraws into you, until
it's over and, when you look up, the group
is wearing the faces of people once again.

Lovers

After orgasm, the lovers are exhausted,
in a shade under which a shawl is sprawled,
a sun-sieved place where others have lain before,
a basketful of fruit beside them. After sex
they're reminded of laundry, chores to do
before light (like a candle withdrawn from a room)
leaves the eye. Eros has no more hold on them.
What keeps them against the world's intent is a ransom
of the heart. And so, they return to those houses
where bodies are ghosts and ghouls behind locked doors,
though their souls are not for pillows or eiderdowns
or sheets; that place is only where they surreptitiously
wait it all out until they can return here to come again,
and empty each other with what their bodies deem
focal, the way breath shifts inside squirming bodies.

On edge

All day the dogs barked—even after the moon
had disappeared into its corner at the back of a cloud,
and no sun had appeared, and it was like the first days
when dust hangs above us after we have put the planet
in a rage over what we do—those dogs just kept barking
through that day. The afternoon stood a while on its toes
pondering the likelihood of a next step. No one
was aware but the sky was full of butterflies fleeing, even
as neighbours cried through the stone wall of their home,
two voices of a thirty-plus-year marriage gone awry. All
afternoon the children played doctor behind the shed:
I could hear them giggling and describing the smells
on their small, reconnoitring fingers, as a late afternoon
storm waited grumpily above, until at the entrance
to evening it broke. I stubbed out my cigarette, yelled
to the kids to come the hell inside. I wanted love to pick up
where it had left off, make you come back and quiet
those dogs; and remove this fear welling up in me.

The detective

I have every evidence of fire in you,
after the smoke has cleared
but embers glare still,
glad as light bugs at dusk.

I can only imagine how you hulled
each other before I arrived,
then hugged and embraced
to keep the trembling,
near your centre of gravity,
smouldering forever.

There's evidence of this.

I'm a detective and see what was done.
I deduce the rest—gasps
in lingering passages, breaths
sucked in, clung on to with teeth—
the soft splosh of tip parting flesh.

These are the aftermath,
grimaces on small-death faces,
the smell of creation in the rooms.

Someone else will study the whorls of fingers
and compare them
to what is on the corpses, on the fridge door,
on edges of the kitchen tabletop
and on the headboard in the bedroom,
where the best of it happened.

The number of dreams

How many dreams,
since I said you were dead,
have you counted?
And in how many of them
could you make the journey
without falling in love,
your patience breached at the seams?
The times I thought you were back,
every night waiting at the door,
but not one symbol of your visit.
Oh, but my body found ways,
many, many ways, sometimes just to kill time,
which it didn't know was undying. Days came
and went like trains looming at great speed
then hurtling past, shaking with a burst
right through my small-town stop.
Such is love and, always, someone
wants it to stay. I have forgotten
the words I never heard you say.
But I'm dying to discover
how many dreams I can live in
and still fall in love with you again.

Three Women

His mother Mary is present,
Her sister, called Mary also
(The wife of Clopas),
As well as Mary Magdalene,
The fiancée of the son of man.
They have all travelled far
To come and see him off.
Before prayers, after which
A chamber must be sealed,
Its wheel-like rock rolled
To block the hollowed out
Side of a mountain, we yank
The lance from his side, wipe
It off, wait for angels to come
And rub his body down, even
As the real criminals twist
Their necks to see the scene.
At his feet, the women weep.
And ponder the reason why
God was killing his only son.

The peace of silence

Now that the scythe sang, and the harvest's done,
bushels and bushels of listless bodies
wait to be stuffed into the quiet soil: I know why
there is a silence to snow, why sheep don't weep.
I am the bottom of an iceberg avoiding yachts,
whole years with voices said edgeways,
never here where earth's rock needs light
in the liquid of a mountain womb. I place my ear
against it to know if the bellyful will ever be born.

Some people know blood as a mountain river
that flows from the Maloti across South Africa
to feed the Atlantic, a roar with a tail
of an eel, and such people smile, lift fists
and praise Koeeoko, the water snake that whirls pools
to make its nemeses eddy with it into mud. We have
no prophets because our last are gone. Long live
the memory of stone in their blood,
their everlasting refusal to crack into meekness.

If happiness has not yet been won, perhaps now
that Maaparankoe is gone the child of his child
will arrive and another wound will be patched. Long
live the melody of the name Mbera although, even when
this happens, no one can know if we will ever be
at ease, in what the ancients call a peace of silence.

The stranger next to me

He sat next to me on a bench in the dark park and said,
'You must live.' The wail of a saxophone told me again
Why I was here tonight, far from the fuss of the city.
I stole a glance at him: his silhouette was smouldering,
The nose, the thick lips of someone who has lived, ears,
He was ablaze but not ready to be put out, his smoke swirling
Around familiar objects, his gaze pieces of coal
From an inferno that refuses to die. My mind clouded with a thought...
When time loses meaning, one avoids the memory
Of people's eyes: I didn't need to look in his to know
The reason for his presence here. You escape history
And construct your own, from a subdued life that can turn
A job, a marriage, into shambles, reflected in people
When they don't know you are watching them.
'Do you have eyes?' I asked, and he laughed with his belly.
When distance disappears, it's time to create more of it to stay alive.
'Yes,' he said, 'Else I wouldn't be here.' He spoke to no one in particular,
Looking ahead like he knew there was something behind the trees
And beyond them the bustle of a city blinking in the night.
I thought of the chortle of a woman I knew, her throat marred by wine,
Laughing aloud every time I came. I still hear myself in her head,
My empty grunts on top of her; she taught me how to move along.
My guest turned to look at me with the holes on either side
Of his nose. His face sizzled at mine. Then he stood up
And left, the way a silhouette swirls into fog. I stood up
And walked carefully toward the lights of the city, calm now
After an evening of thinking about deceit, happy to be alive
Because of someone with no eyes whose name I do not know,
And who had gone back to the inferno where he had come from.

The visiting

A murmuration comes to visit our old days,
its black dots huddled as one, flowing spots
chasing each other from side to side, a school of fish
flying from a predator. We watch it blot the low sky
beside our porch, beyond the top of the height
of an old birch tree. There are silhouettes on the street,
this early in the night, going where shapes go at this hour,
even as sound pauses. Sometimes it'll surge off
and leave without committing to anything violent.
But at other times, swooshing in and out of existence
and blacker than ever it is—it seems—bursting
to speak something to the dusk, a revelation
of some sort; the death of a relative we'd long lost sight of.
It moves like a shoal of black mollies trapped
in a fisherman's net, looking for a way out, dipping
this way and that, then darkens our horizon and puts
unfriendly thoughts in our heads—two old people
out at dusk, on the porch of a small wood house.

When we die

We climb a path to where the spirits of love live,
a spirited life of fire; we feel them hear our approach.
In an imaginary house nearby a presence moves
behind a curtain, a face, as if this place
were the only home for miles with a fierce smell
of musk a body makes during foreplay, and through
the act of sex, into the time immediately afterward
when lovers side by side like each other with the soft,
pink muscle of flesh in their mouths, before the cigarettes
and before rousing each other again with searching fingers.
Throughout the years men who survived death
on the battlefield put their lives on fingers of women.
The house's walls blush with colour at our approach.
A bird takes a bath in a gutter beneath the awning.
At a signal from the sky, flowers stand up, raise
their heads and unfold their arms. It has been a long wait.
The cottage smiles, lets us in, the only people in the world,
because people die when we do this, and that is how
it's always been. We start to remove each other's clothes
button by button till we fill the centre of the room,
neonates always foreign to the idea of what must come.

Whiskey in the jar

In dark-lit pubs at the edges of night
we are hounds baying from the verge
with melodies of the dogs of war
to say in song, and never in writing
nor in long-winded speeches downtown,
why the world is headed back to hell.
We speak with loud poems of malt
through the distances in our look.

> Salt enters the room like raw breath
> and makes its way to the rafters; always
> one more song, one final pint, another way
> to look at a woman who passes by, even
> as the year kills leaves by the millions
> and abandons them on the injured ground,
> then starts making snow in the mountains
> to prepare the harsh winter of winters.

Only then does a love of country
lead one home, where women wait,
love dripping from their hearts
and perfume in between their legs.
You couldn't say that about love, which
has no scent and is known for a different
purpose of grace: to erect castles in the air
and find some way to make them real.

For Peter Horn (1934—2019)

We howled into loudspeakers
stuck to our mouths, hard as chalk
on a blackboard—on an iron rock—
on the things fate forces on us.
On things that face us with our hands
tied. We said *voetsek* to the season
of that month, harsh sandpaper
on skin. We spoke to men with no ears
to tell them it was not the moment
to remove our professor out of time,
men with no eyes, featureless faces,
souls who, we know, keep a strict clock.
We said things that life had fed us,
things on the cutting board of poetry
with ingredients awaiting their turn.
We wriggled, hoped sweat would free
our hands so we could pick up
a book of his, pick a poem hanging
from his marula tree, eat its alcohol.
But the poet left and it's like ripping
a tongue from the mouth of a gulag.
There's death when a sun sinks west
but we know it's coming back, death
when the river dries but leaves wells
on its banks that taste just as sweet,
child wells mourning the Drakensberg.
There is the death of a Cape buffalo
when it charges with its horns low,
like a forklift, and it tosses us up
because it wants a better awareness
from us in future, nature in the ways
of true existence.
                        Peter is that death.

Acknowledgements

Mbera is more than just a collection of poems — it's a project made possible by the generous help of many people, to whom I extend my warmest thanks.

In particular, I would like to thank Robert Berold for his critical insight and expertise in eliminating insincerity. His expertise was indispensable to this work.

Phil Rice of Canopic Publishing for his commitment to this project. Phil's belief in *Mbera* transformed a series of disorganised drafts into the published work it is today.

I would like to thank the magazines, journals and other platforms that published these poems in one form or another. Their role has been crucial.

A big thank you to my family — my wife and children, whose patience has let me devote time to writing.

To my siblings in Lesotho, thank you for the memories that fuel my creativity and remind me of where we come from.

Thank you to Spoken Word Paris, who were the first to hear these poems and give feedback. Your involvement has been essential to my development as a writer.

Finally, thank you to Mbera, Khotsofalang Masilo, our brother, whose spirit lives on in us.

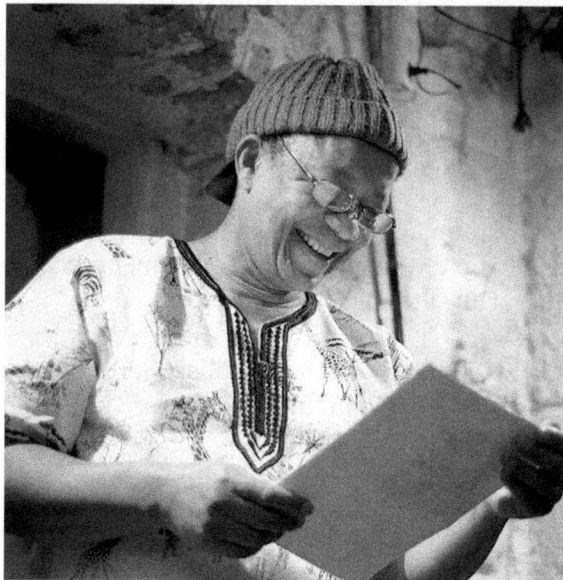

Rethabile Masilo is a Mosotho poet who has lived in Paris, France, since 1987. Born in Lesotho in 1961, he left his country with his parents and siblings and went into exile in 1981. Before settling in France, he lived in the Republic of South Africa, Kenya and the United States of America.

His poetry has been published in various anthologies and magazines. His previous books include *Things That Are Silent* (Pindrop, 2012), *Waslap* (Onslaught, 2015), *Letter to Country* (Canopic, 2016) and *Qoaling* (Onslaught, 2018). He has also edited two anthologies published by The Onslaught Press: *For the Children of Gaza* and *To Kingdom Come (Voices Against Political Violence)*.

Masilo's work is rooted in his experiences of exile and the cultural heritage of Lesotho. His poetry often explores themes of displacement, identity and social justice. He insists that his greatest wish is for his poems to be easily accessible to the Basotho, the people who inspire him to write.

www.ingramcontent.com/pod-product-compliance
Lightning Source LLC
La Vergne TN
LVHW021118080426
835509LV00021B/3433